THE ALPHABET
OF THE
KUKU OF SOUTH SUDAN

LEJU MOGA

RIVER NILE PUBLISHING INC
GRAND RAPIDS, MICHIGAN

ISBN 9780692-79155-4

DEDICATION

This book is first dedicated to my teacher—my mother, who sang to me, and told me several stories that aroused my interest in exploring my social and physical environment from near and beyond.

Secondly, this book is dedicated to my siblings, who read to me stories that took me out of the confines of my village.

Thirdly , this book is dedicated to my school teacher, Mr. Maku, who taught me to write each of the ABCD, in the air, on the sand, and finally in my book; and for telling me that the main difference between a small "B" and a big "B", is that, while a small "B" has only one stomach a big "B" has two stomachs— because it is big.

THE LETTER A

The Kuku letter **A,**
always sounds like the letter **A**,
in the English word **Apple**.

And as in the Kuku word **Ada.**

THE LETTER E

The Kuku letter **E,**

always sounds like the letter **E,**

in the English word **Egg.**

And as in the Kuku word **Kiteŋ.**

THE LETTER I

The Kuku letter **I,**

always sounds like the letter **I,**

in the English word **Ink.**

And as in the Kuku word **Ijiji.**

THE LETTER O

The Kuku letter **O,**

always sounds like the letter **O,**

in the English word **Orange.**

o

And as in the Kuku word **Koloŋ.**

THE LETTER U

The Kuku letter **U,**

always sounds like the letter **U**,

in the English word **Put.**

And as in the Kuku word **Umbölötu.**

THE LETTER Ö

The Kuku letter **Ö,**
always sounds like the —**er** sound,
in the English word **Germ**.

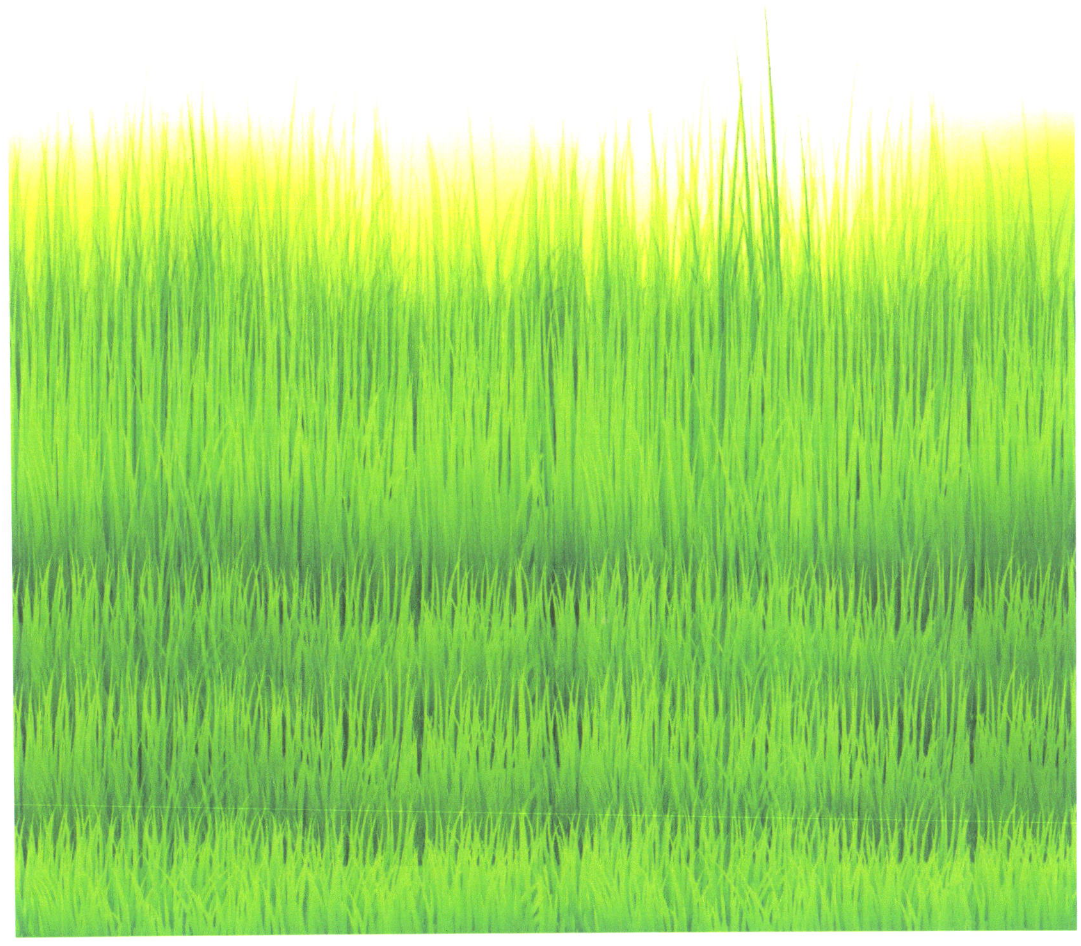

And as in the Kuku word **Döru.**

THE LETTER B

The Kuku letter **B,**

always sounds like the letter **B,**

in the English word **Book**.

And as in the Kuku word **Burukusut.**

THE LETTER D

The Kuku letter **D,**

always sounds like the letter **D,**

in the English word **Dog**.

And as in the Kuku word **Dolotot.**

THE LETTER G

The Kuku letter **G,**

always sounds like the letter **G**,

in the English word **Go**.

And as in the Kuku word **Gorom.**

THE LETTER J

The Kuku letter **J,**

always sounds like the letter **J**,

in the English word **Jug**.

And as in the Kuku word **Jomitat.**

THE LETTER K

The Kuku letter **K,**
always sounds like the letter **K,**
in the English word **Kitchen**.

K

And as in the Kuku word **Kinyoŋ.**

THE LETTER L

The Kuku letter **L,**

always sounds like the letter **L,**

in the English word **Lion**.

And as in the Kuku word **Lodore.**

THE LETTER M

The Kuku letter **M,**

always sounds like the letter **M,**

in the English word **Moon**.

And as in the Kuku word **Maŋga.**

THE LETTER N

The Kuku letter **N,**
always sounds like the letter **N,**
in the English word **Nice**.

And as in the Kuku word **Nore.**

THE LETTER P

The Kuku letter **P,**
always sounds like the letter **P,**
in the English word **Pot**.

And as in the Kuku word **Peta.**

THE LETTER R

The Kuku letter **R,**

always sounds like the letter **R,**

in the English word **Red**.

And as in the Kuku word **Rabolo.**

THE LETTER S

The Kuku letter **S,**

always sounds like the letter **S,**

in the English word **School**.

And as in the Kuku word **Sumuti.**

THE LETTER T

The Kuku letter **T,**
always sounds like the letter **T,**
in the English word **Tree**.

And as in the Kuku word **Tome.**

THE LETTER W

The Kuku letter **W,**
always sounds like the letter **W,**
in the English word **window**.

And as in the Kuku word **Wejetot.**

THE LETTER Y

The Kuku letter **Y,**
always sounds like the letter **Y,**
in the English word **Yam**.

And as in the Kuku word **Yaro.**

THE LETTER ’B

The Kuku letter **’B,**
always sounds like no other letter,
in any English word.

But as in the Kuku word **’Be’be.**

THE LETTER ’D

The Kuku letter **’D,**
always sounds like no other letter,
in any English word.

But as in the Kuku word **’Diko.**

THE LETTER 'Y

The Kuku letter **'Y,**
always sounds like no other letter,
in any English word.

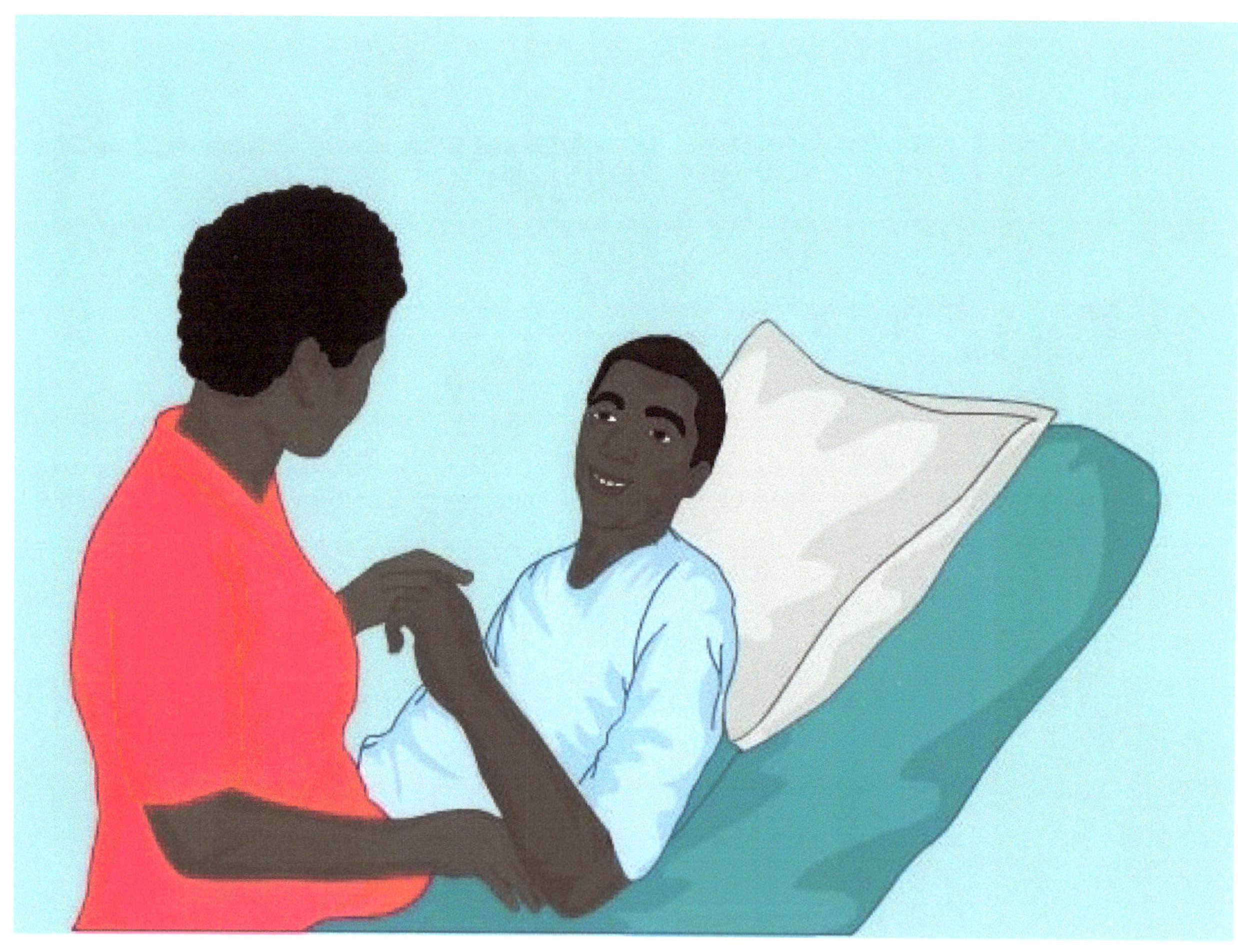

But as in the Kuku word **'Yö'yu.**

THE LETTER Ŋ

The Kuku letter **Ŋ,**

always sounds like the **—ng** sound,

in the English word **King.**

And as in the Kuku word **Ŋiro.**

FORMS OF THE KUKU ALPHABET

THE KUKU BIG LETTERS

A	E	I	O	U	Ö
B	D	G	J	K	L
M	N	P	R	S	T
W	Y	’B	’D	’Y	Ŋ

THE KUKU SMALL LETTERS

a	e	i	o	u	ö
b	d	g	j	k	l
m	n	p	r	s	t
w	y	’b	’d	’y	ŋ

SOME POINTS TO NOTE

Some important points to note about the Kuku alphabet.

There are 24 letters in the Kuku alphabet.

There are six Kuku letters which are vowel letters.

There are 2 Kuku letters which are semi-vowel letters. The semi-vowels letters are the letters Y and W.

There are 18 Kuku consonant letters.

All the Kuku letters must be sounded the same in all words.

There are very few Kuku nouns that begins with a vowel letter.

Any Kuku noun that begins with a vowel letter is a foreign or a defective word.

The letter K is the most common Kuku letter and there are many Kuku nouns which begin with the letter K.

The letters C, F, H, Q, V, and Z are **not** part of the Kuku alphabet. Why? Because their sounds do not exist in the Kuku language.

SUMMARY

A — for **A**da (how?)

E — for Kit**e**ŋ (cow)

I — for **I**jiji (rhino)

O — for K**o**loŋ (sun)

U — for **U**mbölötu (chimpanzee)

Ö — for D**ö**ru (grass)

B — for Burusut (pigeon peas)

D — for **D**olotot (Columbus monkey)

G — for **G**orom (wall)

J — for **J**omitat (Baboon)

K — for **K**inyoŋ (crocodile)

L — for **L**odore (grasshopper)

M — for **M**aŋga (Mango)

N — for **N**ore (band)

P — for **P**eta (tamarind)

R — for **R**abolo (banana)

S — for Sumuti (Fish)

T — for **T**ome (elephant)

W — for **W**ejetot (velvet monkey)

Y — for **Y**aro (hippo)

'B — for 'Be'be (Bridge)

'D — for Diko (cloud)

'Y — for 'Yö'yu (to visit)

Ŋ— for Ŋiro (child)

UPCOMING BOOKS IN THE SERIES

COMING SOON.

IN THE KUKU OF SOUTH GRAMMAR SERIES ARE:

THE PHONICS
OF THE
KUKU OF SOUTH SUDAN

ABOUT THE AUTHOR

Leju Moga was born in South Sudan but now lives in the United States. As a native and someone interested in self learing, he speaks and writes Kuku language very well.

Leju holds a Bachelor of Science Degree with honors. And he enjoys reading and writing in his free time.

www.ingramcontent.com/pod-product-compliance
Lightning Source LLC
LaVergne TN
LVHW070204110826
845147LV00002B/501

* 9 7 8 0 6 9 2 7 9 1 5 5 4 *